T0380862

Song
of the
Seasons

BY:

WILLI FISCHER JED

ILLUSTRATED BY:
SALLY McGREGOR GRAMMAR
AND
WILLI FISCHER JED

For Rob who asked the most fascinating questions
and for Laurie and Tim who listened patiently to the answers.

Copyright © 2010 by Willi Fischer Jed. 532628
Library of Congress Control Number: 2010913605
ISBN: Softcover   978-1-4535-7600-7
            Hardcover 978-1-4535-7601-4
            EBook   978-1-4771-7788-4

Print information available on the last page

Rev. date: 01/07/2020

To order additional copies of this book, contact:
Xlibris
1-888-795-4274
www.Xlibris.com
Orders@Xlibris.com

Song Of The Seasons

As ever, "*Once upon a time*",
This story must begin;
I really don't know why, that's just
The way it's always been.
A little fellow, 'bout your age,
He came and asked his mother,
"Tell me, Mommy, how one knows
One season from another?"

"I know we swim in Summer warm
And roller skate in Spring,
We sled all thru the Winter time,
And Fall's a leafy thing."

"But aren't some other ways
To tell the time of year?
Some other things that happen, too?
It isn't very clear!"

I'll tell you just one story short
About each season, Dear,
Sit down now, very quietly,
A lovely tale you'll hear.

SPRING

In Spring the gentle rain does fall
To wash the new earth clean,
The flowers push the soil away,
The grass turns softly green.

In the foot of our old willow tree,
The little fairies waken;
They call their friends from root to root,
Their winter naps they've taken.

They ask their Mommies, "Is it time
To go outdoors and sing?
Is it the time to dance and play
And make a Fairy Ring?"

A Fairy Ring? Now what is that?
You really want to know?
It's something made by fairy dancers
When there's no more snow.

They come up to the ground each night
And dance around in rings;
The boys are dressed in velvet pants,
The girls in frilly things.

They dance 'til morning sun appears,
Then home they quickly run,
For if they're caught in daylight, they'll
Get freckles from the sun.

And on the spot they disappear,
A very queery thing:
The mushrooms grow a circle round
That's called a Fairy Ring.

And when this ring you see, come dawn,
There's something you will know—
It's Spring, and right here, fairies danced
That came up from below.

SUMMER

In Summer, all the icebergs melt
From off the barren sea,
The whitecaps come and play on her,
The wavelets dance with glee.
The morning sun lights up her face
With orange, pink and bright,
She cuddles and she nestles ev'ry
Grain of sand in sight.

The children come to float on her;
She bounces them around
Like ribbons in a summer breeze;
She is a smiling clown.
The ships, they come from ev'ry land
And ride her sparkling waves;
In shady bays and little caves
She kisses tiny caves
Made by sand crabs - oh! look there
A small and greeny turtle!
(Perhaps her mother, liking green,
Gave her the name of Myrtle.)

It's evening now, the sun hangs low,
It's setting in the West;
This is the time the sea likes best,
The sunset on her crest
Brings forth a rainbow, blue and gold,
The sky is purple pink.
I'd awfully like to be the sea
I really would - I think!

FALL

In Fall, the trees wear golden cloaks
With red and orange streaks.
The little leaves fall down and play
With pebbles in the creeks.

The fieldmice all are scampering
To store up winter food;
The children-mice are helping, too,
They've all been very good.

Then Daddy Mouse, he says to them,
"You've worked so hard all day,
I think it's time you took a rest
And had a little play."

So father mouse, he took a leaf
From off the dripping trees
And made his little mice a boat
As pretty as you please.

While mother mouse made good mouse stew.
The mice, they rode the river,
And father mouse went shopping for
Some hodgey-podgey liver.

The little mice took hankies out,
In which they'd packed their snacks
And ate them on their sailing-ships,
"It's evening! Let's get back!"

Mother sings and stirs her stew
As happy as can be,
While her children hurry homeward through
The leaves so rustle-y.

So keep your eyes wide open, dear,
Especially in the Fall,
When you can see the mice at play,
The happiest time of all!

WINTER

In Winter, laces ride the Wind
And tumble to the ground.
The wind - it is the whist'ling one,
The snow makes not a sound.
Snow, my son, you know about,
The winds you have not met;
There are four kinds, from North and South,
And from the East and West.
The North Wind is the wint'ry one
He wears a hoary beard
Made up of ice and hard-spun snow,
But do not be a-feared.
He's just a kindly giant who
Lives in a mountain cave,
High upon the highest peak
With other winds that wave

He spends his winters howling,
His summers, spends in sleep;
He swirls the snow and paints on it
And piles the snow drifts deep.

At night when we are snug in bed,
He sings his deep, low song,
His lullaby sings us to sleep
And hums on all night long.

When morning comes, he whistles shrill,
"Wake up! Come out and play!"
We go outside to play with him,
He whirls us on our way,

He's cold and brisk and jolly clean,
He sweeps the country side,
He brings an apple-glow to cheeks
And peeps at those inside.

When we come in to the fireside glow
To pop some corn and rest,
We think with a warmth of the old North Wind
And vow to love him best.

You know now how the seasons run,
The secrets each one keeps;
Now snuggle down with pleasant dreams,
Within God's arms to sleep.

Printed in the United States
By Bookmasters